EXPLORING & CUSTOMIZING SIDE NOTES

Blue - exploring sidenotes lead to the pages with additional information.
Green - customizing sidenotes lead to the pages with customizable content.

PICK & APPLY

pages with illustrations are easily numbered

theory pages are mainly located with odd numbers

VIOLET BOOKMARKS
(main themes)

MAIN THEMES &
CUSTOMIZING PAGES

VISUAL MEMORY MATRIX
(last page with images)

how to use it

5

learn to play better

LEARN TO PLAY BETTER

1. when you play **WELL**, you feel **POSITIVE**
2. when you are not playing well, you are not feeling good
3. usually when you are not feeling good, you probably are not going to play well
4. you can learn to change your thinking into **POSITIVE THOUGHTS** and that will allow you to **PLAY BETTER**

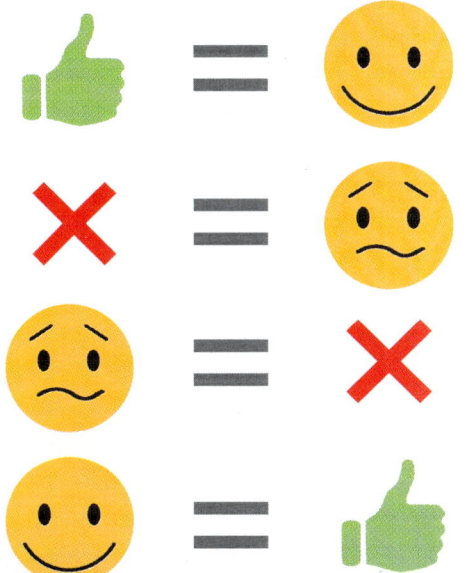

Welcome! Your time has come!

Welcome to the active pocket guide **Pocket Golf Psychology**[tm]. You made a decision to become a better golfer. This book is designed to help you rise in the mental game of golf. Come and discover the uniqueness in yourself as a player!

I.A.M. Golf - Instant Anger Management Golf is a brand new system which supports your abilities and takes your game to the next level. You will learn how to control your emotions and have advantage ahead of the competition. I.A.M Golf means that you can use it immediately, whenever you need.

Customize your game & determine your results by controlling internal balance in an easy and incredibly efficient way.

Advanced mental coaching is specially crafted to be fitted for your skills. It is you who determines your game, your effort, your way, your results. It is you who has control over your freedom. All you have to do is put this book into your pocket and

enjoy the next best swing!

Before reading and applying hints from the book Pocket Golf Psychology, the reader should consider every implication for his / her physical and mental health. Author of this pocket guide does not take any responsibility over actions of individuals that use hints without any reasonable consideration. Every progress in improving mental abilities relies on regular practice with a certified golf trainer.

Performance pocket guide - Pocket Golf Psychology is based on training program Advanced Mental Coaching created by Mario Beky.

Published in 2020 by Mgr. Mario Beky.
Hrádza 83, Michalová 976 57, Slovakia
mail@mariobeky.com
Number of publication 22
Number of edition 1
Printed by MARIOBEKY
Grammar correction Jacqueline Kisova.
Made in Slovakia. UV-2P-STMC
All rights reserved.
Copyright © Mgr. Mario Beky
Graphic design © Mgr. Mario Beky
Print - ISBN 978-80-570-1590-1
EAN - 9788057015901

HOW TO USE THIS GUIDE?

READ IT & USE IT!

We recommend reading the whole publication before putting it in the action. This pocket guide is easy to understand and if you know how to use it, it can save you plenty of time.

The pocket guide - Pocket Golf Psychology provides multilevel user availability for the easiest possible utilization. It's divided into theory, graphics & customizable content (starting on page **58**). Save precious time and find as fast as possible the best solution with advanced searching.

ACCESSIBILITY

This pocket guide offers you several ways how to quickly find useful info anytime you need.

1. Main themes (page **78**)
2. Advanced bookmarking system (**ABS**)
3. Exploring & Customizing Sidenotes (**EX&CS**)
4. List of key phrases (page **77**)
5. Course map indicators (page **76**)
6. Visual memory matrix (**last page - 80**)

You are unique in many ways, so are your searching preferences. Use the one which suits you best.

ABS - ADVANCED BOOKMARKING SYSTEM

advantage

main themes text
in current color code

Outer coloring of the bookmark refers to the color code of pages
gray - generic
blue - exploring
green - customizing

IMMEDIATE RESPONSE

- **immediate response** - active feedback to the new and challenging situation (unexpected, unwanted, difficult) with less rehearsal time and less possibilities to handle it with proper re-action

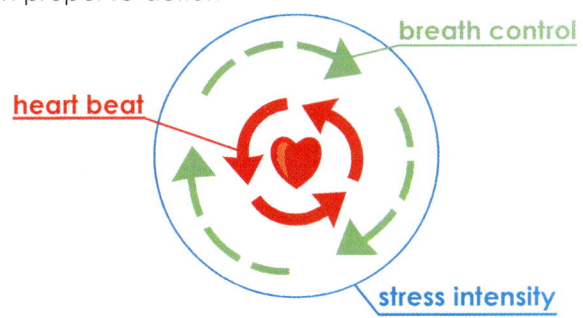

STEP BY STEP BUILD THE FORTRESS OF HEALTHY CONFIDENCE

- try to **immediately control** the stress reaction with **slowing down the process of stress** & reversing it
- in real game (especially in competition) will come up situations that will have the instant impact upon the player
- the more pleasant or difficult situation the more uncontrollable emotional reaction it creates
- the key of handling those types of situations is to be prepared in advance
    1. practice with a golf PRO (to be technically in top shape)
    2. practice the multiple relaxation techniques

immediate response

psychology & golf

PSYCHOLOGY & GOLF
PRESSURE & PERFORMANCE

positive expectations help to retain internal balance

negative expectations increase intensity of pressure

- at home
- practicing or prep. for game
- in the game
- after the game

intensity of physical and mental pressure

time needed for proper preparation for effective mastering stress situation

UNDERSTAND YOUR MIND!

LEARNING TO USE PSYCHOLOGY AS A MENTAL ADVANTAGE!

- using **psychology** means to:
  - identify
  - describe
  - control
    - your **behavior** (and that means):
      - what do you feel
      - how do you act

- always go to the shot or putt with **ONE positive thought**
- always end the shot or putt with **ONE positive thought**
- your thoughts are what is leading your hands and body
- success has 3 pillars – ambition, technique, etiquette
- make sure you are supporting all of them equally

- when you will **learn to strengthen** your **ability to handle stress,** you will need to use less time and energy to be calmed down and return to your state of well-being
- the more you will evaluate the situation with negative expectations, the longer time will be needed for the mental processing ➡ the more unprepared you will be when you'll face the next shot

BEING PREPARED means **BEING ONE STEP AHEAD**

psychology & golf

stress & golf

THINK AND PLAY THE EASY WAY

UNDERSTAND THE ORIGIN OF STRESS & CONTROL IT!

4 anti-stress preparation guidelines:

1st - off course preparation
- auto-regulation, auto-suggestion of positive thoughts

2nd - during practicing
- confrontation with the golf course environment

3rd - short time between shots on the golf course
- active relaxing techniques

4th - after the game
- you are full of fresh experience, review it!

- if you are **shaking, sweating** and your **heartrate has risen,** you are probably facing a situation which your mind(consciously or unconsciously) defined as potentially dangerous
- **stress reactions** are inherited to **protect us** from dangerous situations
- you cannot avoid them but after reasoning, your body can be calmed down - **LEARN TO CONTROL IT**

WHEN A **SITUATION** CREATES A **REACTION,** EXPLORE THE **REALITY,** TRY TO **REASON** AND **RELEASE THE PRESSURE**

1. SITUATION
   - on your way home through a dark street suddenly something BIG and DARK comes out from the shadows (situation thoughts - **you are going to play against a strong opponent** or **facing a shot into rough - water - bunker - forest**)

2. REACTION
   - your hands, legs and whole body starts to shake and your heartbeat goes to 180 bpm in 2 seconds; warmth has prepared the body for RUN or FIGHT (reaction thoughts - **possible humiliation or shot: slice, chunk, empty swing**)

3. REALITY
   - the BIG person is heading towards you, his face is now illuminated with street light and you are recognizing your father (reality thoughts - **when approaching the ball you see that the ball hasn't a bad lie at all**)

4. REASONING / RELEASING PRESSURE
   - (reasoning thoughts - **the ball landed near the water, on the fringe, I can play it!**)

**SOMETIMES BAD SHOTS HAPPEN TO EVERY PLAYER
YOU CAN SAVE THE WHOLE PROCESS
WITH JUST ONE POSITIVE THOUGHT**
(AND WITHOUT ANY NEGATIVE THOUGHT!)

stress & golf

stress & golf

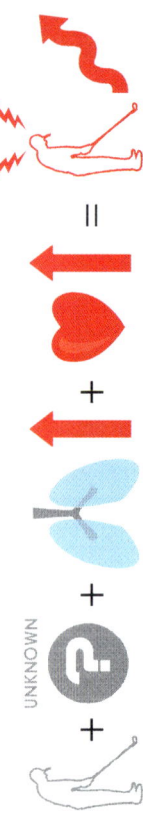

When you're unexpectedly facing the unknown situation your internal security system is getting activated. Breath intensity increases, which rises your heart beat, your muscles start to shake, body warms up rapidly to prepare you for the RUN or FIGHT. Unfortunately that can affect your swing in a bad way.

REVERSE PROCESS OF STRESS

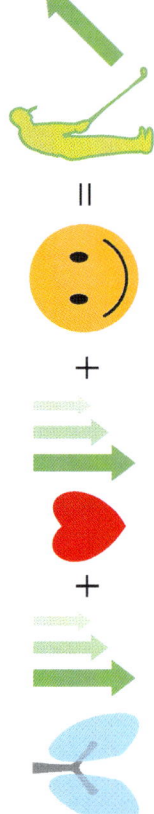

Control the KEY elements and **REVERSE** the **PROCESS OF STRESS** reactions for **YOUR BENEFIT**. Control your breath intensity and calm down your body. Combine relaxing techniques with simple techniques of **POSITIVE EXPECTATIONS**. That can make you a more **SOLID MENTAL PLAYER** and give you **MORE SUCCESSFUL EXPERIENCE** and **MORE PLEASURE IN THE GAME**.

TIME ISSUE MANAGEMENT

- every hole has time for the way it should be played, don't waste your **time & energy!**
- in a moment you are losing time, **your opponents** are gaining time
- with more time, they gain **more self-confidence**, which helps them to be **more successful** - that means you are less successful
- if your opponents are losing time, **you are gaining** it, you are getting more confidence which will help you to be become more successful
- always **think forward with positive expectations**
- you cannot turn back time if hitting an unwanted shot
- all energy taken from an ACTUAL NEGATIVE EVALUATION means saving more energy into the **NEXT POSITIVE APPROACH** from the following shot

OTHER ISSUES MANAGEMENT

- **stress** roots from **many origins** - partner, parents, coach
- motivate yourself to **prepare your mind for a challenge**
- start with acceptance **"I accept to play my best!"**
- it is not what my partner, sponsor, fans want, it is what

I AM PRIVILEGED TO ACQUIRE

- have at least 1 person who gives you **POSITIVE SUPPORT**
- there is never an external factor which influences you, it is always **YOUR THOUGHTS**

---

stress & golf

stress & golf

CLEARING THE VISUALIZATION -
orienting on achieving goals

my GOALS

my decision
my effort
my expectations
my swing
my responsibility

external stirs

shell

sponsor

friends

opponents

coach

partner

family

club members

fans

THE THICKER **MIND SHELL** YOU'LL LEARN TO
CREATE IN THE **CRITICAL MOMENT OF THE SWING**
THE LESS YOU'LL BE AFFECTED BY EXTERNAL STIRS
ON THE WAY TO **ACHIEVING YOUR GOALS**

THE ACTUAL SHOT IS THE MOST IMPORTANT SHOT OF YOUR LIFE

HOW TO MANAGE YOUR THOUGHTS?
**ALLOW YOURSELF TO FOCUS ON ACTUAL MOMENT (SWING) &
YOUR HANDS, YOUR THOUGHTS, YOUR GAME
WILL BE REWARDED**

- focus on actual moment – THIS MOMENT
- you live in **this moment**, you are not living yesterday, not tomorrow, not in 10 minutes, you are living **NOW**
- **YOUR ball, YOUR shot, YOUR trophy** is waiting for you
- it wasn't here yesterday, it won't be here tomorrow
- bomb yourself with **POSITIVE** thoughts & **ENERGY** and **RELAX**!
- if you are confused about your **emotions**, make them **numbers**
  – 10 is top negative, 0 is neutral, +10 is top positive
- some people may push you, don't forget that it is **YOUR EFFORT, YOUR EXPECTATIONS, YOUR GAME**

stress & golf

relaxing techniques

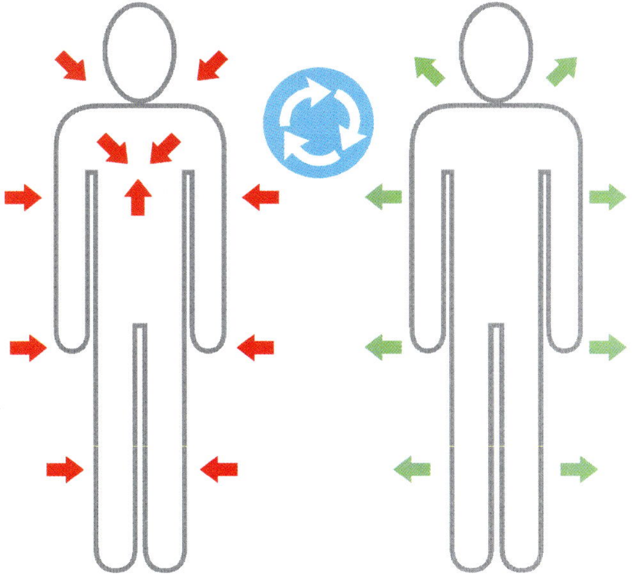

RELAXING TECHNIQUES

RELAXING BEFORE PRACTICING

- you can do it on the couch or in the car seat

1. **apply** medium **pressure** on muscles of your whole body or just one part of your body for **2 seconds**
2. **release** the pressure for **2 seconds**
3. **repeat** each session but **not more than 3 times consecutive** (with every new session increase time by 2, by 4, by 6 sec.)

RELAXING BEFORE PRACTICING

- practicing is a KNOWN situation
- you know what to expect, therefore you can be **better prepared**
- **mental relax = physical relax**
- renew, restart positive memory

- use **autosugestive thoughts** (goals) which should be

> **POSITIVE, SPECIFIC & ACHIEVABLE:**
>
> - **I CAN** do it!
> - Today is **MY DAY!**
> - Today I will play a **GREAT ROUND!**
> - I have practiced very hard for this!
> - I will chip, putt and drive **LIKE NEVER BEFORE!**

- avoid NEGATIVE THOUGHTS or thoughts with any negative content like:

- I will not fail.
- There will be no bogeys on my scorecard.
- I did not practice much, hopefully it won't harm my game.
- I cannot lose any stroke.
- I hope I will not make many mistakes.

relaxing techniques

relaxing techniques

- Consistency is more than distance!
- I didn't put marker in my bag!
- BALANCE YOURSELF!
- FLY! GET OFF MY NOSE!
- Watch your grip!
- I should practice more!
- Rhythm is Monte-Carlo!
- Just don't hit the water!!!

TUNNEL OF ATTENTION

| 1st memory sector | 2nd memory sector | out of attention |

time continuity

RELAXING BEFORE THE GAME

- **prepare** yourself **in long term** especially when you are thinking about your career in golf
- consult your health with professionals
- leave yourself a time reserve
- make a **list of things** that you will carry **in a bag** when practicing and when going into competition

RELAXING AFTER THE SWING

- **your result is determined** - how you think 3 to 10 seconds before swinging and 20 seconds after swinging the ball with the club
- you have **enough time to think** about the swing but never enough time to spare on other issues
- you have to practice your **internal swing autopilot** - every thought which is needed to make the swing must be set free
  - **execute** everything learned **without thinking** about it

The tunnel of attention

- circle of thoughts - your thoughts go in circles - **FIRST info IN, FIRST info OUT** - (1st thought of series of thoughts which enters the attention is the one which is also first forgotten)
- you probably know it from your personal experience when you are repeating phrases in time of leaving home or office "I must have - phone, keys, glasses... phone, keys, glasses..."

relaxing techniques

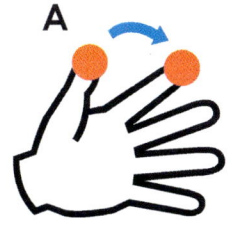

1. inhale approx. 30% of your lung capacity for 2 seconds
2. use connection between thumb and index finger as reference point A

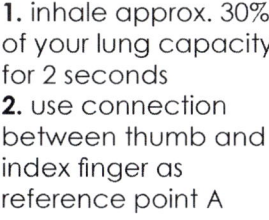

↑ 1/3 ↑

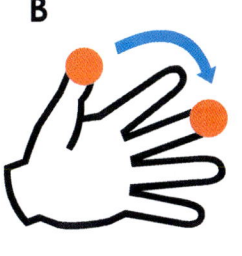

3. inhale approx. 60% of your lung capacity for 2 seconds
4. use connection between thumb and middle finger as reference point B

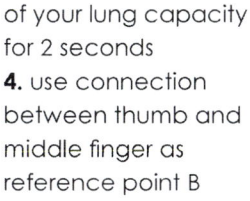

↑ 2/3 ↑

5. inhale full capacity of your lungs for 2 seconds
6. use connection between thumb and ring finger as reference point C

↑ 3/3 ↑

Use this exercise in situations in which you need to calm down quickly without necessary attention.

RELAXING AFTER THE SHOT

- **your next step will depend:**
  50% - on how you encountered the stroke
  50% - on your playing attitude
- if you are losing control over your emotions, remember to return to the basic theory of stress
- otherwise adrenaline level can ruin your scorecard
- always do:
  - **realistic reasoning**
  - **positive oriented evaluation**
- manually lower the intensity of pressure, stress (read more instructions on page above)
- breath intensity control – reverse process of stress

I DON'T WANT TO RUN AWAY,
I WANT TO FACE IT,
I WANT TO UNDERSTAND IT,
I WANT TO CONTROL IT,
I WANT TO WIN!

If you want to learn more about staying calm under pressure and achieving the best personal performance, join the Ultimate Mental Game Training in Mario Beky Academy

relaxing techniques

rethinking

RETHINKING
THE MENTAL APPROACH

-1 < -2 > E

birdie isn't better than EAGLE, but is better than PAR

E < -1 > +1

par isn't better than BIRDIE, but is better than BOGEY

+1 < E > +2

bogey isn't better than PAR, but is better than DOUBLE BOGEY

+2 < +1 > +3

double bogey isn't better than BOGEY, but is better than
TRIPLE BOGEY etc.

RETHINKING THE MENTAL APPROACH

- if you are not satisfied with actual results it is time for **REASONING AND REVIEWING** MISTAKES & FAULTS
- **YOU HAVE TO PRACTICE WITH a golfing professional** at least once a month
- the golf PRO is looking at your swing from the other side
- if you feel confident on the driving range but you don't **deliver scores in tournaments** maybe you should consider playing at least 1 risky shot per round
- when playing a tournament, **reconsider**,
  sometimes the GAIN is worth of the RISK
- **play a LOT to learn** to recognize **DECIDING MOMENTS**

RETHINK THE MENTAL APPROACH & DO THE MATH
every time you are feeling pressured
and you don't know how to continue

- the difference between the next worse shot are always 2 strokes, 2 REASONS how NOT TO RUIN the whole SCORECARD (with making bad shot increases probability of hitting the next bad shot multiple times)
- BUT! if you are not a goldenchild and the tournament you are actually playing is not the US OPEN, try to change your thinking **from RISKY to REASONABLE**
- your game is highly specific, therefore IF your clubs are custom fitted for your body & game level, why don't you **fit your mental game to play your best?**

rethinking

cognitions

COGNITIONS & GAME OF GOLF

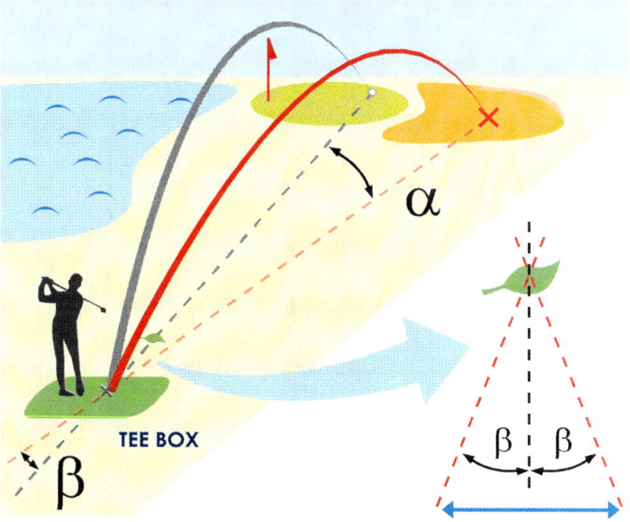

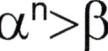

AIM FOR THE SPOT WHERE YOU WANT TO PLACE YOUR SHOT!
The way you aim determines (usually),
the final position of the ball.

You can move the ball on **BLUE LINE** according to
reference point to adjust direction of ball flight.

$$\alpha^n > \beta$$

If you don't make a correct adjustment to BETA
degree ALFA mistake will be multiple times bigger.

- **cognitions** are processes by which the sensory input is transformed into your mind
- cognitions help you **transform** all received **data into language** that your **mind will understand**
- recognizing processes would start over and over again, therefore our mind uses stored data which is similar to what we see, sense, feel and experience - these data are sometimes called **anchors**
- anchors **help** our brain to **categorize** and compare **similar information**

    for example – we look at a map of Italy as a boot
- **golf** has a lot of similarities which are used as anchors:

  to divide a swing into 2 exact time halves for example using the term such "Monte-Carlo", "Puerto-Rico", etc.

  to read directions on the fairway, on the green use different color of grass, different shapes of leaves

  for reading direction on the driving tee, we cannot use any help to find proper way to the point of the dropping zone but we can move our ball position according to any visible thing, such as divot, broken tee, etc.

  use everything natural for getting flight information on the golf course; many objects are usable also for measuring height and dropping ground – poles, sticks, water, branches, grass, rocks, bridges, etc.

  JUST PLAYING WITHOUT REHEARSAL IS PURE GAMBLING

cognitions

THREE PILLARS OF SUCCESS

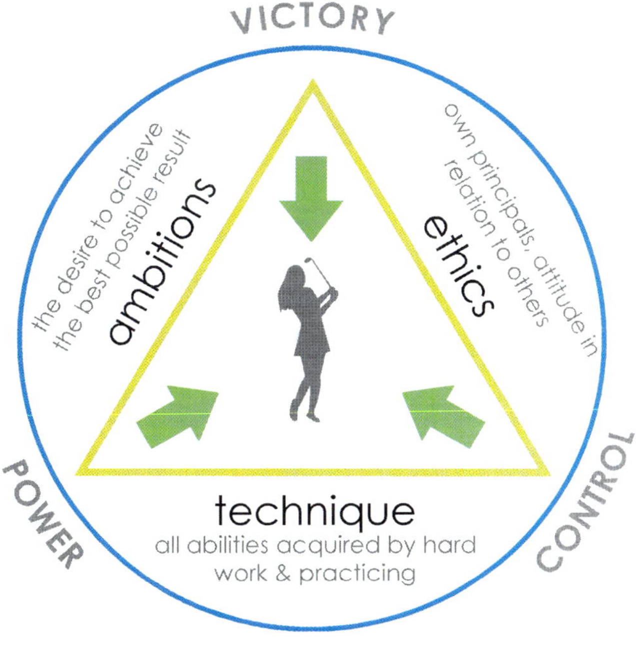

VICTORY

the desire to achieve
the best possible result

ambitions

own principals, attitude in
relation to others

ethics

POWER

CONTROL

technique
all abilities acquired by hard
work & practicing

**YOU ARE THE PLAYER IN THE MIDDLE OF THE TRIANGLE
AND IF YOU WANT TO BE SUCCESSFUL,
YOU NEED TO WORK ON THESE THREE PILLARS EVENLY
OTHERWISE YOU WILL LOSE THE BALANCE**

CLEAR VISION

- to not be affected by **external stirs**, you have to **clear your visualization** - "remove the stirs"
- if your coplayer, coach, partner, course, country, sponsor are origins that affect your game in a negative way, change them
- ignoring external stirs is never an easy process, because we are sensitive beings
- you need plenty of

PATIENCE AND SPECIFIC GOAL

Healthy game confidence required following specifics:
- **summarize your goals** and set yourself a goal before you are going to practice, or play a round
- when you don't pick a goal, you don't have direction where you want to go - you're either A. moving forward or B. you're moving backward
- make sure your goals are **semi difficult**
- watch all three pillars of success closely:
    - **etiquette**
    - **ambitions**
    - **technique of the game**

POWER + CONTROL = VICTORY

- make sure that you work on every one of them with the same amount of energy and attention
- if one of 3 pillars fades, you will lose balance and fail

cognitions

advanced practicing

ADVANCED PRACTICING TECHNIQUES

INTENSIVE - SHORT GAME

- perfecting the short game boosts your **playing confidence in the game**
- **practice with** a teaching **golfing PRO** at least once a month for your short game

- in the approach to every putt, remember that **distance is** always **the key factor** - after this, everything else
- distance varies on many conditions:
  - **type of turf**
  - **time of the year, season, day**
  - grass is **changing direction** during the day
  - **humidity of the grass**
- accept the fact – no matter how hard you try, you cannot achieve a **perfect result in putting** average, you can just **get close**
- work hard on **the most important golfing statistics** – TO GET CLOSE TO 1,00 putts per hole (by relatively consistent statistics FIR - fairway in regulation and GIR - greens in regulation)

PUTTING CONDITIONS #1

- SUN, WIND, DRY, FAST
- MORNING, AFTERNOON, SLOWER
- RAIN, SLOWEST

GREEN OR PRACTICING GREEN

advanced practicing

PUTTING CONDITIONS #2

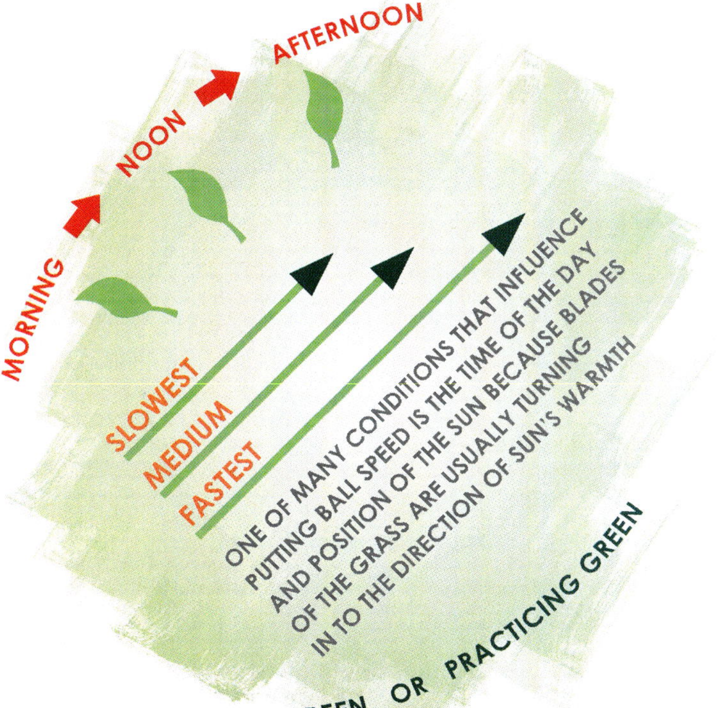

advanced practicing

GREEN OR PRACTICING GREEN

ONE OF MANY CONDITIONS THAT INFLUENCE OF MANY CONDITIONS THAT INFLUENCE OF THE DAY AND POSITION OF THE SUN BECAUSE BLADES OF THE GRASS ARE USUALLY TURNING IN TO THE DIRECTION OF SUN'S WARMTH

FASTEST
MEDIUM
SLOWEST

MORNING
NOON
AFTERNOON

PUTTING CHIPPING & CHIPPING DISTANCE PRACTICING

advanced practicing

advanced practicing

PUTTING DISTANCE PRACTICING

- reading greens is much more easier with technical equipment like **contrast glasses**
- reading shapes of greens is very important when you are aiming to improve your game, however

DISTANCE IS THE DECISIVE FACTOR

- control your **mind awareness in distance control** with this simple **PUTTING DISTANCE EXERCISES**:
- practice **from a longer distance to a shorter distance**
- first make a shot from 15 yards, 10 yards, 5 yards; use own distances eg. 15 meters, 10 meters, 5 meters etc.
- try multiple variations 12 feet, 9 feet, 6 feet, 3 feet or use own system eg. 3 meters, 2 meters, 1 meter etc.
- set yourself **smaller goals first**, then ask for more
- "I have to hit 5 times in a row."
- **DO NOT TOLERATE MISTAKES**, if you are not 100% effective, start all over again
- it will take hours, days, weeks, months but you will **PUTT BETTER THAN THE REST** of the playing field
- learn to know the distances of clubs in your bag

CHIPPING & PITCHING DISTANCE PRACTICING

- use a similar strategy as with putting when **chipping, pitching and bump & run shots**
- it **can be modified** in more ways than putting, because of larger variety of clubs that can be used

CLUB YARDAGE/METERING

	normal swing	power shot	punch shot		
D	_____ **yds/m**	_____ yds/m	_____ yds/m	driver	....°
W	_____ **yds/m**	_____ yds/m	_____ yds/m	... wood	....°
W	_____ **yds/m**	_____ yds/m	_____ yds/m	... wood	....°
H	_____ **yds/m**	_____ yds/m	_____ yds/m	hybrid	....°
H	_____ **yds/m**	_____ yds/m	_____ yds/m	hybrid	....°
2i	_____ **yds/m**	_____ yds/m	_____ yds/m	2 iron	....°
3i	_____ **yds/m**	_____ yds/m	_____ yds/m	3 iron	....°
4i	_____ **yds/m**	_____ yds/m	_____ yds/m	4 iron	....°
5i	_____ **yds/m**	_____ yds/m	_____ yds/m	5 iron	....°
6i	_____ **yds/m**	_____ yds/m	_____ yds/m	6 iron	....°
7i	_____ **yds/m**	_____ yds/m	_____ yds/m	7 iron	....°
8i	_____ **yds/m**	_____ yds/m	_____ yds/m	8 iron	....°
9i	_____ **yds/m**	_____ yds/m	_____ yds/m	9 iron	....°
PW	_____ **yds/m**	_____ yds/m	_____ yds/m	Pitching W.	....°
SW	_____ **yds/m**	_____ yds/m	_____ yds/m	Sand Wedge	....°
LW	_____ **yds/m**	_____ yds/m	_____ yds/m	Lob Wedge	....°

advanced practicing

advanced practicing

PRACTICE - PLAY TO THE FLAG

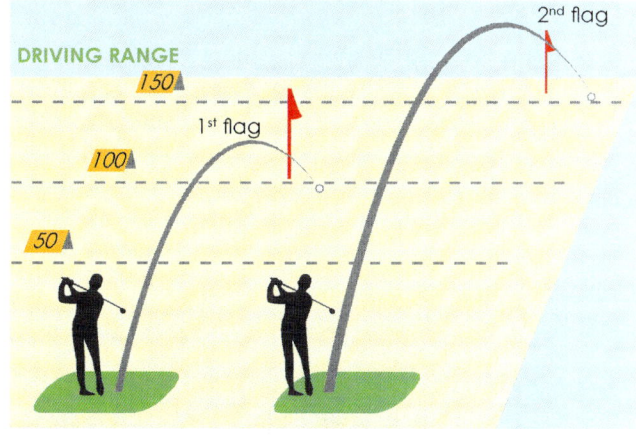

ADJUST TO YOUR LEVEL OF GAME

I. Example of practice **PLAY TO THE 1st FLAG**

1. STROKE - 60° wedge
2. STROKE - 56° wedge
3. STROKE - 50° wedge
4. STROKE - pitching W

II. Example of practice **PLAY TO THE 2nd FLAG**

1. STROKE - pitching W
2. STROKE - 9 iron
3. STROKE - 8 iron
4. STROKE - 7 iron

Customize with your system of units eg. yard, meter.

DON'T FORGET TO PRACTICE WITH A GOLF PRO!

PRACTICE - PLAY TO THE FLAG

- this exercise is best for **short and medium distances**
- **modify** it to make it useful and comfortable **for your game level**; it can be executed for example like this:

- pick the **first flag on the driving range**, usually 50 yards or 50 meters
- it will work even better with huge basket as many of driving ranges provide this opportunity
- take **3 or 4 shortest clubs** out of your bag
- try to shoot to the flag with every club with **only 1 shot**
- moderate swings to **shoot with different clubs every time at the same distance**
- set yourself (first smaller) a goal to shoot 50, 60, 70, etc. times out of 100 shots close to the flag (in the basket)
- when shooting, **take your time** for rehearsal and let your body relax; think about the next shot

> ALWAYS THINK ONLY ABOUT NEXT SHOT
> **BECAUSE YOU WILL NEVER HAVE OPPORTUNITY TO REPAIR SHOT FROM THE PAST**

- use alignment rods or spare clubs for correct orientation on the target
- don't forget to practice with a golfing PRO from time to time to make sure your swing is correct

advanced practicing

advanced practicing

PRACTICE - VIRTUAL PLAY

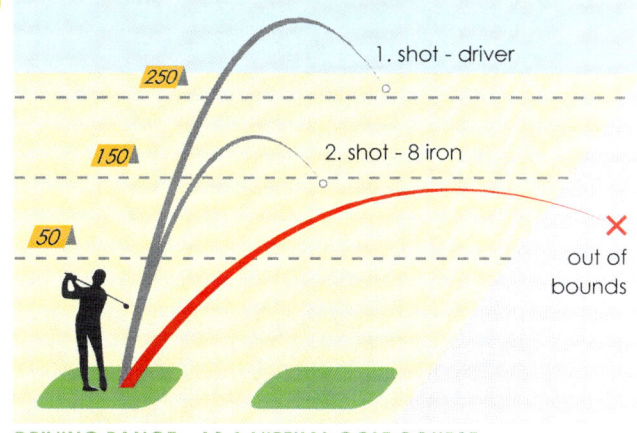

DRIVING RANGE - AS A VIRTUAL GOLF COURSE

ADJUST TO YOUR LEVEL OF GAME
Example of practice **PLAY VIRTUAL PAR 4**
380 yards/350 meters LONG

1. STROKE - driver
2. STROKE - 8 iron
3. STROKE - won't be played because if you hit over 250 - yards/ meters, you'd probably need only a shorter iron to get to the green. So after the second stroke you will switch to the next **virtual hole.** If you will hit virtually even out of bounds, you add a stroke to your **virtual scorecard** according to the rules and eg. drop the ball. Customize with your system of units.
25 seconds per stroke | 50 balls in the bucket

PRACTICE - VIRTUAL PLAY

- 67 this practice is FANTASTIC as a preparation for an important tournament
- you must have the **birdie book/yardage book** of the golf course you want to play virtually will give you correct distances of holes
- 68 you can **fill the birdie book** before or along practicing with important notes or use the example table on p. 68
- play all shots on the driving range **as it would be on a real golf course**, with exception of putting
- play the golf course virtually just in your head, you don't have to walk anywhere; play on driving range
- you have **no mulligans**
- one bucket of 50 balls should be enough
- always **take only 1 stroke**, if play is incorrect, make imaginative drop, add stroke and play the next shot

MENTAL PREPARATION

YOU ARE THE RULER OF YOUR TIME

- rehearsal - you will have a certain amount of time to completely play a hole and use it all if you need
- you have approximately 20 – 25 seconds for 1 stroke on a normal golf course
- don't be hasty, **make yourself comfortable** and then proceed to shot
- give yourself a time reserve for easing up after an unwanted shot because in a **real game it will be tough**

advanced practicing

mental strategies

STRATEGIES FOR THE GAME OF GOLF

HOW TO FOCUS ON SUCCESSFUL SETTING AND ACHIEVING PREDETERMINED GOALS

INTENSIVE - SHORT GAME

- focus your concentration on PRIMARY goals
- remember, that you don't have to think about them in your actual game
- **make a hierarchy of** these **goals** fitted for yourself
  * you can do it alone or with a golf PRO
- every **new goal** should be a little bit **higher** than your actual level of playing

EVERY GOAL SHOULD BE **SPECIFIC AND ACHIEVABLE**

- set a **certain a time to accomplishment** a specific number **of goals**
- **for achieving** every **goal**, give yourself a small **gift** - this will **motivate** you to want and do more

YOU CHOOSE THE PATH, YOU SHAPE THE RESULT

- on the following pages, you can find examples of how your list of goals will look like:

GLOBAL STRATEGY FOR ACHIEVING A GOAL #1

Player **without a handicap** (goals for one month)

- 10 or more practice sessions with a golf PRO
- play two 9 hole rounds with a golf PRO

Player with a **handicap 54** (goals for one month)

- play first handicap tournament
- play two 18 hole free rounds
- 5 practice sessions with golf a PRO

Player with a **handicap 54 - 25** (goals for one month)

- play 2 or more HCP tournaments
- play two or more 18 hole rounds
- 2 or more practice sessions with a golf PRO
- play 2 rounds with **90** or less strokes
- play **40%** or more FIR (fairway in regulation)
- no more than **3.5** putts per hole average

mental strategies

 **mental strategies**

GLOBAL STRATEGY
FOR ACHIEVING A GOAL #2

Player with **handicap 25 - 10** (goals for one month)

- play 2 or more handicap tournaments
- play two or more 18 hole rounds
- 2 or more practice sessions with a golf PRO
- play 2 rounds with **80** or less strokes
- play **50%** or more FIR (fairway in regulation)
- no more than **3.0** putts per hole average

Player with **handicap 10 or less** (goals for one month)

- play 2 or more handicap tournaments
- play two or more 18 hole rounds
- 2 or more practice sessions with a golf PRO
- play 2 rounds with **75** or less strokes
- play **60%** or more FIR (fairway in regulation)
- no more than **2.5** putts per hole average

ACTIVE STRATEGY FOR ACHIEVING A GOAL

- **73** set FOR yourself an ultimate golfing goal:
  – to play PAR, or to get close, or play better
- almost all golf courses are designed to be played in PAR for every player's specific level of game
- if you are not disabled in anyway, you should be able to play PAR
- you can play the regular PAR as well
- regular practicing with a golfing PRO is a MUST on the way to the PAR game
- a golfing PRO is a person who will show you not only the way to play better, he will detect and repair mistakes you make in a swing
- **64** you must play a lot to **get to know your game and understand, what are for you, the most important goals in your** active **strategy**
- **42** strategies for achieving a goal can help you organize steps for improving your game and not to think about unnecessary thoughts which may hurt your score
- don't forget to prepare on the first stroke of the first hole because this moment can determine how you will proceed during the whole round
- don't wait until tomorrow,

YOUR MOMENT IS NOW

- **43** explore examples of active strategy stages:

mental strategies

41

mental strategies

ACTIVE STRATEGY
FOR ACHIEVING A GOAL

To play the best shot, you don't need jackets or jugs to play a correct shot. All you need is a clear mind. When a king goes into battle, he never wears a crown.

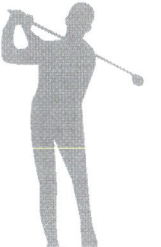

When facing a shot, put down all trophies and other unnecessary thoughts.
Stand barefoot with only 1 thought - **SIMPLE SWING** and you will perform a **PERFECT SHOT**.

1 swing

2 **regulation**

3 PAR

4 **PAR 72**

5

5 STAGES TO APPROACH A WIN

5th stage goal

- set yourself a **BIG goal**, to win a specific MAJOR, name it, **make a picture in your mind** that you are receiving a trophy; make a place for it, or prepare a special hanger for the GREEN JACKET, make sure that you see it every time you practice and every time you come back from a tournament;

LET IT REMIND YOU:

"I HAVEN'T REACHED IT YET!"

4th stage goal

- set a goal to play a **PAR (72)**; if you want to compare yourself with excellent golf players, you need to **achieve this score**; once you achieve it, you can tell that you have set a new standard for your game -
"THIS IS MY STANDARD. I CAN PLAY IT. I CAN PLAY IT REGULARLY."

mental strategies

mental strategies

3rd stage goal

- when facing a new hole, set yourself a goal to **PLAY PAR** on it; it is not that difficult, you know that you already hit a drive over 250 yds / 230 m and you have already played green on PAR 4 with a 2nd shot,

  "I CAN DO IT AGAIN, I CAN DO IT WITH A SMILE!"

2nd stage goal

- when facing a new hole, set yourself a goal to play every shot in **REGULATION**;

  "FAIRWAYS ARE WIDE, GREENS ARE PLAIN, MY GRIP IS STRONG, MY MIND IS CLEAR!"

1st stage goal

- when facing a shot, FORGET ALL GOALS and don't think about any of them; all you need to do is go back to the fundamentals

  GRIP, STANCE, RHYTHM

IF YOU ARE THINKING IN THE MOST INTIMATE MOMENT
ABOUT ANYTHING OTHER THAN YOUR CLUB AND THE BALL
YOU ARE CHEATING YOURSELF ON YOUR GAME

THE MOST INTIMATE MOMENT OF THE GAME

PAR 72 | PAR | **FIR/GIR** | swing

1-putt
green in regulation
fairway in regulation

ONLY 1 POSITIVE THOUGHT

SIMPLE SWING

The jacket is on the rack, the trophy is on the shelf, the PAR score will be shown on the leaderboard, but before you'll get on the green through the fairway, first you must take a swing.

mental strategies

45

game play routine

GAME PLAY ROUTINE

ADVANCED FORMS
OF GAME PLAY ROUTINE

22 • the more you lower your HCP, the more you will try to avoid risky play because you know that **EVERY SHOT IS PRECIOUS**

• one of the key elements in progress in the mental game of golf is to **allow yourself to be better**

• to be better means to accept actual **best performance as YOUR GAME**

• in moment you achieve your new best score so far, try to play it repeatedly as many times as possible

54 • next step to be a **better mental player** goes through acceptance - achievement of score PAR is your own game,

YOUR NEW STATUS

• if you will try to divide your games into those which are played just for fun and games which are more important, make sure, that every playing encounter determines your **progress or regress** in the game

• be ready to **control your self confidence** because it is possible that lack of self confidence will try to convince you that a better score was just pure coincidence

- actively **REACT ON YOUR EXPECTATIONS**, needs and results as this will create your **GAME PLAY ROUTINE**
- when you are practicing, try to remember what practicing technique made you **play better in the last round**
- although golf is called a game - in serious game (competition) **there are no friends, just opponents**, just rivals; when starting a new round, shake their hands with respect but let them know with your eye contact that **you are not giving any round up for free**
- watch your game, record your success **step by step**, put trophies even those small ones, on a shelf somewhere where you can see them everyday
- compare data of your game = they can give you a lot priceless information about yourself and about your mind
- **let your game be evaluated** but only with a player who is better than you - a golfing professional is the most appropriate person to do so
- the more you play this game, the more you are going to look at it as science:
    - the more you can identify
    - the more you can describe
    - the more you can control
        - what do you feel and how do you act

game play routine

game play routine

ICARUS* ACTIVITY APPROACH

BALANCE YOUR SWING / BALANCE YOUR CONFIDENCE

OVER EXCEEDED EXPECTATIONS

TOP break down zone (thin line)

STRONG FOCUSING
on achieving predetermined goals

HEALTHY GAME CONFIDENCE

LOOKING FOR EXCUSES
blaming on external factors

BOTTOM break down zone

NEGATIVITY, LACK OF CONFIDENCE

 maintaining the average level of healthy game confidence can guarantee you steady results, constant strengthening of confidence can give you more opportunities of **WIN** - see the **3 pillars of success**

YOU FLY TOO HIGH - YOU'LL BURN
YOU FLY TOO LOW - YOU'LL DROWN

* from the classic Greek myth of Daedalus and Icarus

PRE-TOURNAMENT WARM UP

- **warming up** - before a competitive round (tournament) it is a important part of game play routine
- use the next examples or create your own warm up routine

PREPARE YOUR MIND AND BODY IN ADVANCE

- relax before entering the golf course
- the best way to avoid making an unwanted shot at the first hole is to **have time reserved** for stretching & driving range practice; eg. +/- 30 minutes
- to learn how to stretch body muscles in the proper way always contact a licensed professional, otherwise you'll assume the risk probability of an injury
- always **start with shorter** distance shots which require smaller tension to your muscles
  eg. 3 x 5 yards, 3 x 10 yards, 3 x 30 yards etc. or 3 x 5 meters, 3 x 10 meters, 3 x 30 meters etc.
- never hit the first practicing shot with the club with more than 50% of your power
- the goal of hitting not more than 5 shots per club is just to renew the memory that stores the movement info
- usually there is no need to empty the whole bucket of DR balls - **you want to warm up your muscles** & not getting tired
- you don't need to think about other players on the DR
- make sure to reserve a 10 minutes warm up for putting - **putting is the most important part of game**
- try to find the **best balance and rhythm for yourself**

Victory is always a priority, but never a goal, because
YOU CAN NEVER LOSE A TOURNAMENT, ONLY THE SWING

game play routine

game play routine

EACH GAME IS AN EXPERIMENT

- watch conditions under which **you are successful** & pretend to be a scientist, it's fun and it's useful
- if you will recognize (**identify, describe and control**) conditions of your success at one place, you will be able to use them **anywhere you will need**
- if you don't know them yet - you will
- golfing professionals should be able to help you to **find your game routine**
- the more data you gain (the more you play), the stronger results you will obtain - and re-use
- modify **possibilities and conditions** under which you play until you will be successful
- use every one of your games for comparing gathered data
- one of the most obvious reasons of not-winning is that golfers play with golf clubs not-fitted for their game
- ask a golf professional or a local store for these options
- another common issue is that players expect to be great in every aspect of the game - modern history of golf shows us that there are golfers who were better drivers, better putters, better mental players, etc.

YOU MUST FIND WHAT YOU ARE BEST AT

ADJUSTING VARIABLES

IF YOU will play number of shots under PAR, or PAR while playing a regular round with appropriate field of players (which will be a better result in continuity comparing to other non regular rounds) **without stimuluses that are limiting your potential, eliminate or lower their influence**

- if you play **the best round of your life** without music bumping through your headphones, **DO NOT** ever listen to it while practicing on the DRIVING RANGE
- if you play **the best round of your life** without father who is pushing you to get better results everytime **DO NOT** ever take him with you for practicing, nor for a tournament
- if you play **the best round of your life** without lucky charm, talisman, favourite cap, which was given to you as a birthday gift from your wife, **LEAVE IT** at home
- if you play **the best round of your life** without any unnecessary thoughts about the game performance, **LET THEM GET OUT OF YOUR HEAD** forever
- if you play **the best round of your life** without... any other THING which you did not ever need throw away everything what is preventing you to

game play routine

game play routine

PRACTICE WITH GOLF PRO!

- after you **work hard enough** to get the result of this psychological experiment which you could be able to repeat, practice with a golfing PRO even more than you have practiced before
- knowledge of the stronger or the weaker aspects of your game will help you to tell the PRO more specific indications to the next step

ONE VERY IMPORTANT THING

you must understand and ACCEPT that it is not likely to **reach 100% rate of success**

- take it easy next time and don't waste energy on blaming stupid clubs, balls, course, weather because maybe it's just not your day
- there are many variables and most of them are external; you have only **one STEADY POINT** – creating your own playing routine - **a gameplay corner stone**
- there is an immense need for you to practice with a golfing professional
- IF YOU ARE NOT progressing with one golfing PRO, switch to another
- maybe one day it will be your **score card** which will be **engraved in silver**

SELF-CONFIDENCE

BELIEF, CREED
AS A PSYCHOLOGICAL FACTOR IN THE GAME

belief in yourself, belief in victory - 2 ways:

A conscious or nonconscious orienting on securing conditions which could **rise the possibility of a victory** as high as possible (professional guidance, healthy life style, time management etc.)

B belief that you can hold on to other forces other than your own - talismans, lucky charms, etc., **anything but not your own ability**

- these items are used as powerful and intensive self-motivating objects which reject negative thoughts and possible endings of a desired action
- belief, creed can be a fantastic & tremendous HELP, BUT it can destroy your **healthy self confidence** in the moment when you have given every bit of your investment to achieve specific goals
- in the moment of the use of external factors you may choose - to hold on either to something which is virtual or scientifically validated

self-confidence

REMINDER

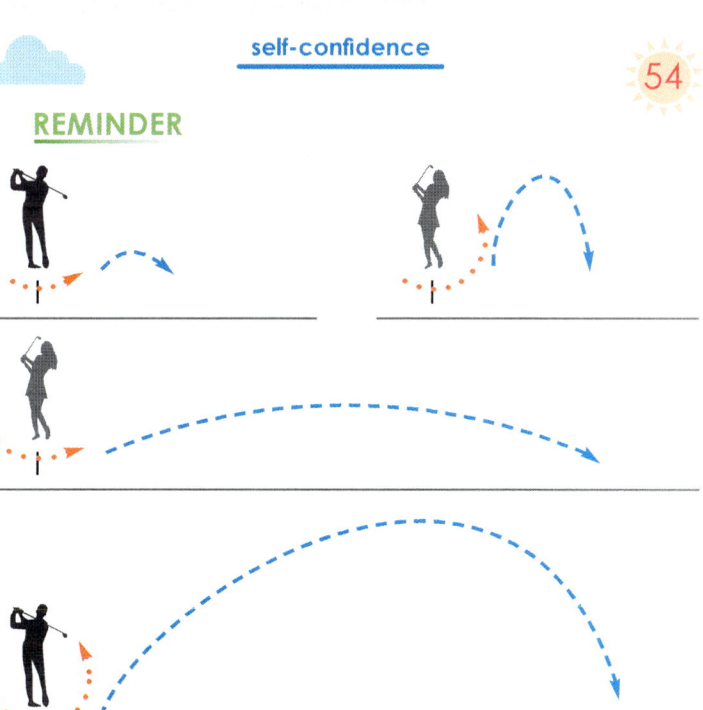

higher spin, flight

average spin, flight

lower spin, flight

The stressful situations arise from time to time. We start to feel pressured because we don't know how to continue. Our subconsciousness pushes us to avoid this pressure so we make quick decisions. These decisions we wouldn't make under normal conditions. Here are some basic rules (how to execute the swings) we tend to forget when our fear tries to defeat us.

YOU ARE THE ONE

- psychological pressure moments which are coming during play have no origin in quality towards your opponent or the deep rough which has eaten up your ball and certainly not from non-functional lucky charms
- psychological pressure rises in your head with your thoughts, your initiative (mostly non-conscious) and

YOU ARE THE ONLY ONE WHO CAN CONTROL IT

self-confidence

MIND, POWER & CONTROL

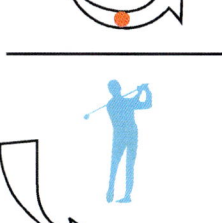

- it is your mind that controls the power added to your arms during the swing (power by total vs. partial intensity)
- it is your hands that create rotation & path of the club
- it is the club that dictates the trajectory of the flight of the ball
- it is the landing point of the ball which creates the emotions - **positive**, **neutral** or **negative**
- practice a lot & practice with golf PRO to find connection on the journey from mind control to desired emotion

identify, describe & control

To understand the natural path of the swing try to swing with weight on a string. Feel the motion that is created and transform it to your golf swing. You'll soon find that you don't need to use lot of power to get more distance.

MIND MUST BE BALANCED
RHYTHM MUST BE BALANCED
SWING MUST BE BALANCED

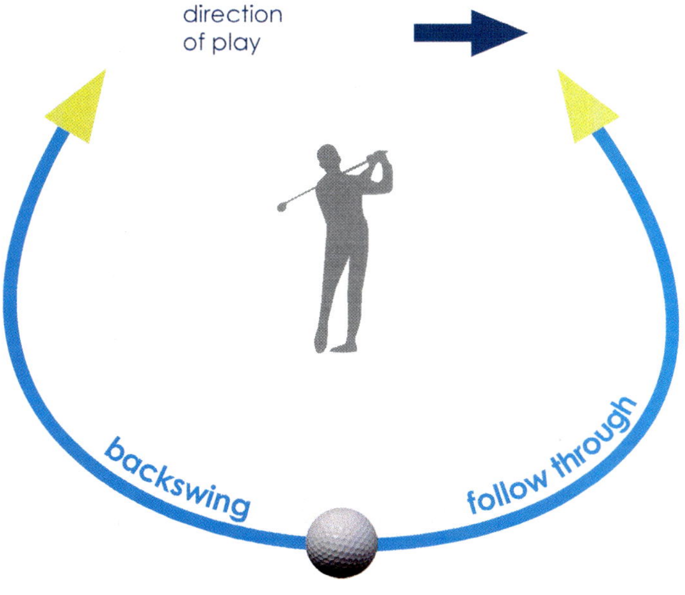

direction of play →

backswing   follow through

example **Monte-Carlo**

backswing and follow through - to remain the same time interval, use 2 easy to remember words of two syllables

self-confidence

mental game achievements

TROPHY CASE OF MENTAL ACHIEVEMENTS

Win all ☐
trophies

- practice with golf PRO, play, compete & get to the crown of all trophies
- enjoy your progress when checking the achievements

1

sub PAR ☐
play sub PAR round

2

Play PAR ☐
score in 18 hole round

3

Recovery 1 ☐
2nd round better than 1st round

4

Recovery 2 ☐
save score from bad numbers

5

1st WIN ☐
MATCH PLAY

6

bogey free round ☐

7

1st BIRDIE ☐

8

1st EAGLE ☐

9

1st ACE ☐

10

1st 60%+ ☐
FIR & GIR

11

1st WIN ☐
tournament away course

12

1st WIN ☐
tournament home course

13

1st PAR ☐
on hole

14

no double bogey round ☐

15

no triple bogey round ☐

Best round score   95 ▶ 90 ▶ 85 ▶ 80 ▶ 75 ▶ 74 ▶ 73 ▶ 72 ▶ PAR

3 YOUR MIND

What are the 3 most precious thoughts that you allow to enter into your mind in last seconds **before THE SHOT?**

You need no more than 3 thoughts in critical situation. FREE YOUR MIND!

free your mind

Write down the most common thoughts you have when you're facing the shot. Reduce them 3 times so at the end you'll have just 3 most important of them. This will make your choice easier when facing real challenge.

SCORECHART #1

Fairways in regulation

FIR / indicator

seasonal FIR
previous	actual

indicator / season

Greens in regulation

GIR / indicator

seasonal GIR
previous	actual

indicator / season

Brutto score (BS) / strokes to PAR

score / indicator

seasonal BS
previous	actual

indicator / season

---

example FIR, GIR % | **indicator**
| 71,4 → | ← 71,7 |

indicator depends on how you played previous HCP tournament

Keep tracking your best monthly score from handicap tournaments. Record FIR, GIR and brutto score so you can see your progress or regress.

RECORD, INTERNALIZE & PROGRESS!

scorechart

SCORECHART #2

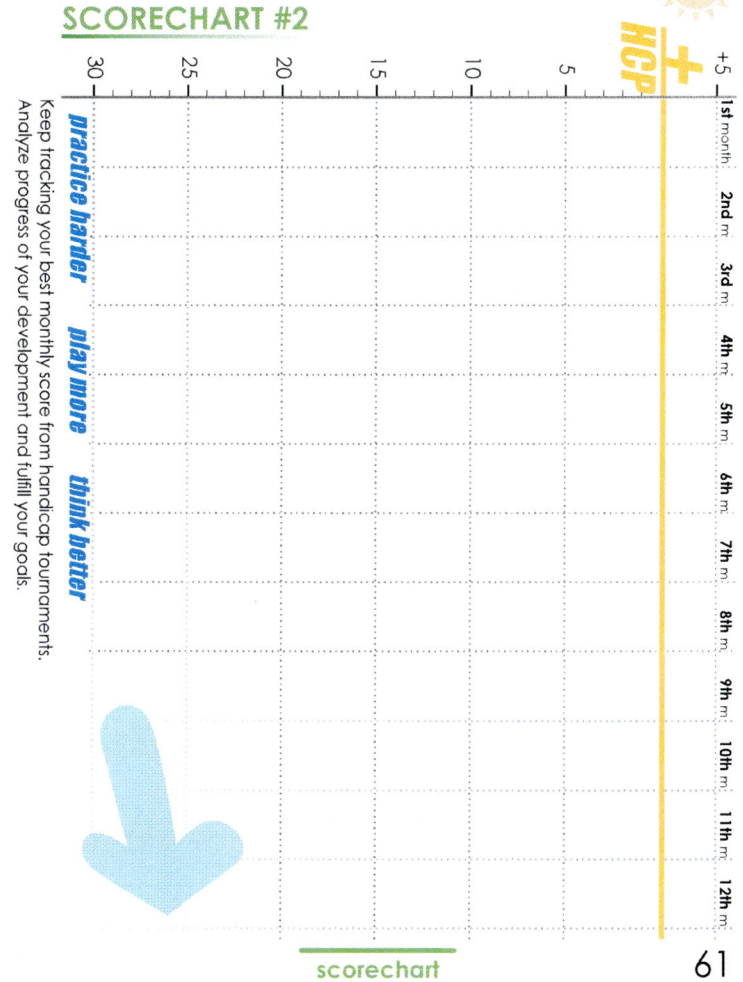

practice harder   *play more*   *think better*

Keep tracking your best monthly score from handicap tournaments. Analyze progress of your development and fulfill your goals.

scorechart

in the bag checklist

Practicing BAG

- long game clubs
- medium game clubs
- short game clubs
- putters
- balls | gloves
- accessories
- practicing aids

Competition BAG — MAX. 14 CLUBS IN BAG

- ☐ driver
- ☐ woods
- ☐ hybrids
- ☐ irons
- ☐ putter
- ☐ balls ☐ gloves ☐ eyewear
- accessories
- marker ☐ ballmark repair tool ☐ tees ☐ pencil
- rain equipment
- umbrella ☐
- ☐ membership card / green card

CONTROL YOUR "IN THE BAG CHECKLIST" IN ADVANCE!

IN THE BAG CHECK LIST

GOLFING GOALS

- write down your golfing goals for a year in advance
- goal should be specific & achievable
- set a certain a time to accomplishment every goal on the list
- for accomplishing every goal, give yourself a small gift

I choose the path & I determine the results!

goal	date
goal	date
goal	date
goal	date
goal	date
goal	date
goal	date
goal	date
goal	date
goal	date

golfing goals

custom global strategies

64

CUSTOM GLOBAL STRATEGY
FOR ACHIEVING A GOAL #1

39 Player **without a handicap** (goals for one month)
STAGE 1 - achieved in ___ month/s ◯

◯ __ or more practice sessions with a golf PRO
◯ play ___ 9 hole rounds with a golf PRO

Player with a **handicap 54** (goals for one month)
STAGE 2 - achieved in ___ month/s ◯

◯ play first handicap tournament
◯ play ___ 18 hole free rounds
◯ ___ practice sessions with golf a PRO

Player with a **handicap 54 - 25** (goals for one month)
STAGE 3 - achieved in ___ month/s ◯

◯ play ___ HCP tournaments
◯ play two or more 18 hole rounds
◯ ___ or more practice sessions with a golf PRO
◯ play 2 rounds with ___ or less strokes
◯ play ___% or more FIR (fairway in regulation)
◯ no more than ___ putts per hole average

CUSTOM GLOBAL STRATEGY FOR ACHIEVING A GOAL #2

Player with **handicap 25 - 10** (goals for one month)

STAGE 4 - achieved in ___ month/s ◯

- ◯ play ___ or more HCP tournaments
- ◯ play two or more 18 hole rounds
- ◯ ___ or more practice sessions with a golf PRO
- ◯ play 2 rounds with ___ or less strokes
- ◯ play ___% or more FIR (fairway in regulation)
- ◯ no more than ___ putts per hole average

Player with **handicap 10 or less** (goals for one month)

STAGE 5 - achieved in ___ month/s ◯

- ◯ play ___ or more HCP tournaments
- ◯ play two or more 18 hole rounds
- ◯ ___ or more practice sessions with a golf PRO
- ◯ play 2 rounds with ___ or less strokes
- ◯ play ___% or more FIR (fairway in regulation)
- ◯ no more than ___ putts per hole average

custom global strategies

practicing plan

PRACTICING PLAN A

• write down your practice plan, it will help you set your direction

date	long game
	short game
date	long game
	short game
date	long game
	short game
date	long game
	short game
date	long game
	short game
date	long game
	short game
date	long game
	short game
date	long game
	short game

PRACTICING PLAN B

- write down your practice plan, it will help you set your direction

date	long game
	short game
date	long game
	short game
date	long game
	short game
date	long game
	short game
date	long game
	short game
date	long game
	short game
date	long game
	short game
date	long game
	short game

practicing plan

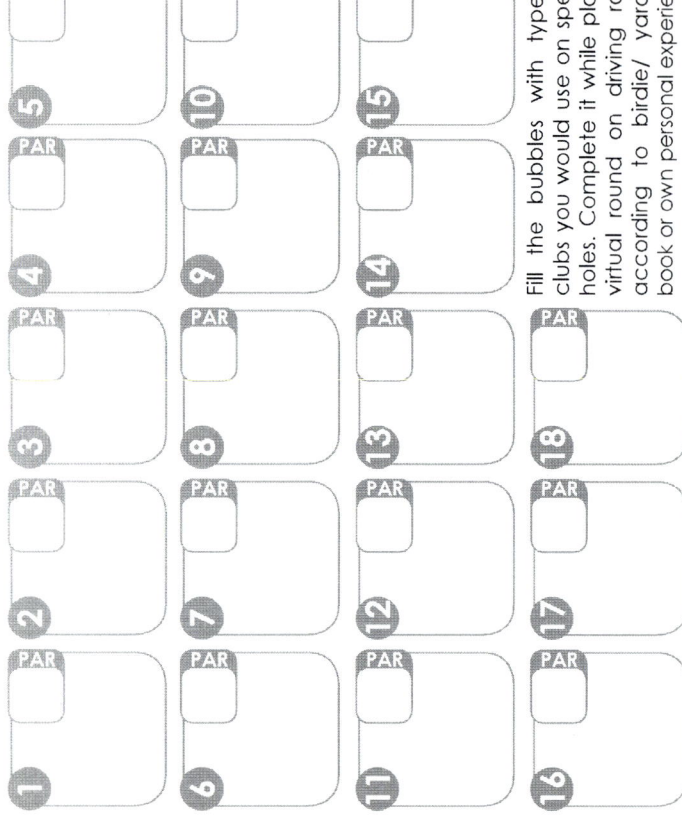

CUSTOMIZE THE VIRTUAL PLAY PRACTICE 2

Fill the bubbles with types of clubs you would use on specific holes. Complete it while playing virtual round on driving range according to birdie/ yardage book or own personal experience.

golf course

tee

par

custom virtual play

LIST OF MISTAKES

Record mistakes you make during the game so you don't forget them. Return to them after and work hard on correcting them. **Repair & never repeat!**

- ⬜ _____ fixed
- ⬜ _____
- ⬜ _____
- ⬜ _____
- ⬜ _____
- ⬜ _____
- ⬜ _____

- ⬜ _____ fixed
- ⬜ _____
- ⬜ _____
- ⬜ _____
- ⬜ _____
- ⬜ _____
- ⬜ _____

Pick the toughest ones which made you practice harder & play better after the correction

list of mistakes

70

PRACTICE WITH A GOLF PRO - CALENDAR

_____   _____ ○
      issue/name of the golf PRO   date

_____   _____ ○
      issue/name of the golf PRO   date

_____   _____ ○
      issue/name of the golf PRO   date

_____   _____ ○
      issue/name of the golf PRO   date

_____   _____ ○
      issue/name of the golf PRO   date

_____   _____ ○
      issue/name of the golf PRO   date

_____   _____ ○
      issue/name of the golf PRO   date

_____   _____ ○
      issue/name of the golf PRO   date

_____   _____ ○
      issue/name of the golf PRO   date

_____   _____ ○
      issue/name of the golf PRO   date

_____   _____ ○
      issue/name of the golf PRO   date

_____   _____ ○
      issue/name of the golf PRO   date

- this Practice with a golf PRO calendar will help you to watch your practicing routine and issues you're working on in a time table

practice with PRO calendar

evaluation

EVALUATION

- from last competitive round of golf write down:
  1. what made you feel good
  2. what made you feel poorly
- compare both evaluations & mark the one which exceeds **+** or **-**

CUSTOM ACTIVE STRATEGY - THE GOAL OF ALL GOALS

1. _____

2. _____

3. _____

4. _____

5. _____

Create your own Active strategy for achieving your ultimate goal. Rethink, analyze and calculate all possibilities that should lead you to your ultimate goal.

May you achieve your Goals & Dreams!

custom active strategy

MY POSITIONS IN TOURNAMENTS

rankings

Nr.	position	score	date	name of the tournament/golf course
1.				
2.				
3.				
4.				
5.				
6.				
7.				
8.				
9.				
10.				
11.				
12.				
13.				
14.				
15.				

INDEX OF KEY PHRASES

ABILITY - 9, 12, 45, 66, 68, 70, 72

ACHIEVING - 45, 58, 63, 64, 66, 68, 71, 72

APPROACH - 48, 56, 64, 68, 71

BEFORE THE GAME - 49, 59, 62, 63, 70, 71

CONFIDENCE - 58, 63, 68, 71, 72

CONTROL - 33, 45, 53, 54, 56, 60, 68, 71

COURSE MANAGEMENT - 56, 66, 68, 71, 72

DISTANCE - 33, 54, 56, 68, 71

EMOTIONS - 6, 7, 8, 9, 11, 12, 14, 27, 51, 53, 55, 56, 59

IMMEDIATE RESPONSE - 6, 7, 18, 19, 20, 22, 27

IN DA GAME - 7, 12, 13, 14, 15, 20, 22

MENTAL STRENGTH - 15, 63, 64, 66, 68, 71, 72

MOTIVATION - 6, 63, 64, 66, 70, 71

ON THE TEE - 6, 33, 45, 56, 62

POWER - 45, 53, 66, 68, 71

PRACTICING - 28, 29, 30, 31, 34, 35, 36, 37, 52, 66, 68, 71, 72

PRE - TOURNAMENT - 49, 62, 63, 64, 68, 71, 72

PREPARATION - 62, 64, 68, 70, 71, 72

PRESSURE - 6, 20, 22, 59, 68, 70, 71

RE - THINKING - 53, 54, 56, 63, 66, 68, 70, 71, 72

REASONING - 11, 14, 15, 56, 63, 71, 72

RELAXING - 6, 16, 17, 19, 20, 21

RHYTHM - 54, 56, 57, 71

SCIENCE - 8, 9, 28, 29, 30, 31, 33, 50, 51, 61, 72

STRATEGY - 38, 39, 40, 41, 42, 43, 44, 56, 63, 64, 68, 71, 72

STRESS - 8, 9, 42, 45, 48, 54, 55, 59, 67, 71, 72

TRAJECTORY - 33, 54, 57, 58, 68, 71

UNWANTED / UNEXPECTED SHOT - 6, 7, 20, 22, 68, 71

VICTORY - 6, 45, 53, 56, 60, 64, 68, 71

key phrases

main themes

WELCOME

HOW TO USE IT — 4

PLAY BETTER — 6

IMMEDIATE RESPONSE — 7

PSYCHOLOGY & GOLF — 8

Pressure vs. time 8 | Psychology as a mental advantage 9

STRESS & GOLF — 10

Origin of stress 10 | Situation, reaction, reasoning 11 |
Reverse process of stress 12 | Time & other issues management
13| Clearing the visualization 14 | The most important shot 15

RELAXING TECHNIQUES — 16

Relaxing before practicing 17 | Tunnel of attention 18 |
Relaxing before the game/swing 19 | Relaxing after the shot 22

RETHINKING OF MENTAL APPROACH — 22

Better calculations 23

COGNITIONS & GOLF — 24

Three pillars of success 26 | Clear vision 27

ADVANCED PRACTICING TECHNIQUES — 28

Putting conditions 29 | Distance practicing 31 | Club metering
33 | Play to the flag 34 | Virtual play 36 | Mental preparation 37

MENTAL STRATEGIES — 38

Focusing on achieving predetermined goal 38 | Global strategy
39 | Active strategy 41 | 5 stages to approach a win 43 |
The most intimate moment of the game 45

GAME PLAY ROUTINE — 46

Icarus activity approach 48 | Pre-tournament warm-up 49 |
Game is an experiment 50 | Adjusting variables 51 | Practice
with golf PRO 52

SELF-CONFIDENCE — 53

Belief, creed as a psychological factor 53 |Reminder 54 |
You are the one 55 | Mind, Power & Control 56 | Balance 57

YOU'LL GAIN MORE — 75

PROFESSIONAL WAY
OF TRACKING YOUR VICTORIES

course map indicators

COURSE MAP INDICATORS

on the green

③¹ ②⁹ ③⁰ ②² ²⁰ ¹⁸

⁵⁶ ¹⁷

⁴⁵ ⁵⁴ ¹⁵

²⁵ ¹⁴

green
in regulation

²² ¹²

¹⁵ ⁶ ⁷

down the
fairway

¹⁴ fairway
in regulation

to the green

¹³ ⁷ ¹¹ ¹² ¹³ ⁵⁶

¹²

¹¹ ⁵⁶

⁶ ⁵⁵

hazard situations

⁵⁴

⁶ ¹² ²¹

after the tee shot

⑥ ⑪ ⑫ ㉑

⑧ ⑬ ⑭ ⑰ ㊽

before the game
/to the tee

⑥ ⑭ ⑮ ⑲ ㉔ ㉕   ㊾ ㊿ ⑤⑤

on the tee   ㉛ ㉜ ㉝

⁵⁷ ⁵⁶

⁵⁵

⁴⁵

- visual system of integrated hints for practicing
- numbers indicate on which pages you can quickly find info related to the main topic
- for example for practicing mental game situations after the tee shot, go to pages 6, 11, 12, 21